MW00471099

BEAUTIFUL SAD EYES

Also by r. h. Sin

Whiskey Words & a Shovel
Whiskey Words & a Shovel II
Whiskey Words & a Shovel III
Rest in the Mourning
A Beautiful Composition of Broken
Algedonic
Planting Gardens in Graves
Planting Gardens in Graves
  Volume Two
Planting Gardens in Graves
  Volume Three
She Felt Like Feeling Nothing
Empty Bottles Full of Stories
She Just Wants to Forget
Falling Toward the Moon
We Hope This Reaches You in Time
A Crowded Loneliness
She's Strong, but She's Tired
She Fits Inside These Words
Winter Roses after Fall
Dream, My Child
Anywho, I Love You
I Hope She Finds This
Come Back to Me
This Day Is Dark

**ALSO BY
ROBERT M. DRAKE**
Chaos Theory
Star Theory
Light Theory
Moon Theory
Beautiful and Damned
Gravity: A Novel
Seeds of Chaos
Beautiful Chaos
A Brilliant Madness
Black Butterfly
Broken Flowers
Spaceship
Science
Beautiful Chaos 2
Dead Pop Art
The Great Artist
Moon Matrix
Seeds of Wrath
Dawn of Mayhem
The King Is Dead
Empty Bottles Full of Stories
Falling Toward the Moon
She Fits Inside These Words
Winter Roses after Fall

r. h. Sin

BEAUTIFUL SAD EYES

Robert M. Drake

Andrews McMeel
PUBLISHING®

ROBERT M. DRAKE
contents

ROBERT M. DRAKE

WHEN YOUR LIFE FLASHES BEFORE YOUR EYES—WHERE DOES THE LIGHT GO?

We all have
that one person

we wish
we could have fought

a little harder for.

Spent
a little more time

with.

That one person.
That one decision

that changed
everything for us.

We all have
that one person
who will forever
cling to us.

Who will forever
be the one
who got away.

This is our truth.

But nonetheless
we learn

how to put
that person behind us.

We learn
how to live

without them.

How to love
without them.

We learn
how to be

ourselves again.

We learn
how to move on.
How to heal.

How to look back
at the past

and smile
at everything that's happened.

Both the good
and bad.

We appreciate
the time we had

with them
and learn

from our mistakes.

People change.
People grow.

Strangers become lovers.

And lovers become strangers
all over again.
And we,
as lovers,

have that one stranger
we wish

we could have held on to
a little longer.

Perhaps then

everything would be different.
Perhaps then

our lives
wouldn't be the same.

And wouldn't be
so difficult,

after all.

SOMETIMES WHEN YOU HEAL OTHERS
YOU ALSO HEAL YOURSELF

On the twenty-third day
of November,

I got a message
from a young lady.

She was asking for help.
It seemed

that she had run
out of options.

It seemed

that she had no one
left

to help guide her.

To help
point her toward

the right direction.
She said
she was in a terrible

narcissistic relationship.

That she had been trying
so hard

to move on.

That she had been trying
so hard

to let go.

"Good evening.

*I realize that you receive
many*

*thousands
of Instagram messages,*

*but
just in case
you read this . . .
I wanted you to know
that your beautiful words*

are truly
helping me to heal

(grieving the loss
of my dad . . .

and my relationship,
which was not my choice).

You have helped me
find my

self-esteem,
self-confidence,
and self-worth.

I am a clinician by profession
but embarrassed

and ashamed
that I stayed in a gaslighted,

narcissistic relationship
for so long.

A huge thank you!

Appreciate and love your mind

and words," she said.

It took me a few days
to respond.

But I knew
I wanted to say something.

I was just thinking
about what I could say

to motivate her.

To help her.
To steer her toward

the light.

To give her some
sort of inspiration.

On the twenty-ninth day
of November,

I wrote back.

Took me long enough
to find the words

I needed to say.

*"I'm sorry about your dad.
I really am.*

*I know what that's like
to lose someone*

*you'd always thought
would always*

be around.

*With time,
things will get better,*

*but I know
losing him will create
this small void
that you won't ever*

be able to fill.

That's life, you know.
A part of it.

And we must understand that.

Life is cruel sometimes.
About your boyfriend,

that is also a shame.
It is hard

to move on
from someone

you love, too.

It is hard
to let go.

Even if you know
with every fiber
in your being
that they are no good

to you.

*People stay
because they feel as if*

they must.

*They feel as if
there is nothing left
to run to.*

*Love is a lot like that.
It makes you blind.*

*It blurs everything
around you.*

*The possibilities.
The opportunities.*

Etc.

*It even makes you believe
that you will not
find*

a better relationship.
A better love.

But there are endless
possibilities

out there.

An endless amount
of people

to form new relationships with.

So sometimes I ask,
Why is it, really,

that we stay?

Is it for them?
Is it for us?
For you?

It's hard to move on.
I know.

*Especially when
you've given so much*

of yourself.

*It is also
very hard*

to start over.

*To even think
about giving someone else*

*the same amount
of love*

and energy.

*That thought
can be overwhelming.*

So I understand why people stay.

*Because of fear.
The uncertainty.*

The belief that maybe
they won't find

better.

But they will

if they allow themselves
to let go.

If they allow themselves
to move on.

And at
their own pace, too.

No one deserves
to be

in a narcissistic relationship.

No one deserves that.
So it is up to you.
To take that step.

To learn how
to let go.

To learn how
to adapt on your own.

Without the need
for that toxic person.

Baby steps.
Little by little.

Start small.
Believe me.

The outcome will be greater
than you think.

Be fearless."

She wrote back a few hours later.
And to my surprise,

she barely said anything in return.
She just said,

"Thank you."

And for some reason,
I felt as if I had moved

the earth with one breath.

I felt
as if the tip

of the universe had leaned
over me . . .

and, alone
in my cold room,

I quietly said
to myself . . .

"Thank you, too."

WHEN YOU FEED SOMEONE THE LIGHT OF YOUR SOUL, THEY, TOO, CAN SHINE

I was having
a bad night.

I couldn't sleep.
I couldn't calm down.

My anxiety
was eating me alive.

I logged on to Facebook
and scrolled down

and opened the first message
I saw.

It said.

"'I had nights
where I had a gun

pressed against
my head.

Nights
when I just
wanted to end it.

When I would wake up
in the middle of the night

in tears.

When I would find
myself

in the middle of my day
and out of nowhere
feel

even more alone.

Nights when
I would spend

countless hours
talking to people

who cared about me
and left me

even more empty
than before.'

That was one
of the last things

my brother told me
before he passed," she said.

"And now I feel
as if

I'm headed toward
the same path.

And I'm stranded.

I'm struggling with it all.
I feel like I'm suffocating.

I feel unheard.

I feel misunderstood.
I feel alone.

I feel broken.

As if a part of me
has been lost,

and
it is never coming back.

I feel angry.
I feel sad.

I feel like crying
and laughing
at the same time," she added.

It was hard for me
to muster any words.

It always is
when someone talks to me

about losing someone
they love.

It's not an easy thing
to open up about

and not an easy thing
to listen to.

Considering all the pain
she's gone through.

I mean,
who am I to comfort her?

And with what?
My own misery?

I don't think so.

I couldn't even understand it
myself.

So who am I
to try to translate that

into someone else's
problems?

But I get it.

People need to vent.
People need

to open the windows
of their souls

from time to time.

To let things air out.
To let things

they've been holding on to
be carried away
by the wind.

I understood that.

*"Don't ever put yourself
in that position again.*

*Your life
is far more valuable
than you know.*

Even in your darkest moments.

*Your life
is far more valuable
than you know.*

*Even when you think
you can't move on.*

*Your life
is far more valuable
than you know.*

*Even when you think
you have nothing else
to live for.*

*Your life
is far more valuable
than you know.*

*Always,
always remember that,"* I said.

Of course.
Perhaps.

Those were not
the right words.

Of course.
Perhaps.

I said the wrong thing.

But
at that very moment

that was all
I could think of.

That was all
I had.

I wish I had more.

"You saved me," she replied.
a few minutes later.

And that was
the end of it.

Sometimes you just need
someone to tell you

how important
you are

without them
really knowing who you are
to begin with.

Sometimes you just need

someone,
anyone,
who understands.

Who has been there
and who has walked through hell
and made it out

alive.

Sometimes that's all you need.

Someone to tell you
all the things

you already know
but also

all the things
you want to ignore.

Stay beautiful, my friends.

Stay free.

WHEN THE UNIVERSE USES PEOPLE TO CONNECT WITH OTHERS ... IT ALL MAKES SENSE

*"I'm convinced
there are times*

*you are writing
only for me!*

*This one
is no exception,"*

she said.

Of course,
perhaps

this might not be true.

But who knows!
Sometimes

things like this happen.

Sometimes
it is a poem.
A movie.
A moment.

A gesture.
Anything, really.

And it always happens
at such

a perfect moment
in your life

that all you can think
and feel

is
as if

it is happening only
for you

to experience.

And sometimes it's so
strangely

connected to you
that it seems

as if
it is nearly impossible

for it to be
a coincidence.

Because it is not.

The universe has
a strange way of speaking

to you.

Of letting you know
you're not alone.

Of letting you hear
what you need

to hear

in order to make it through
your next journey.
Listen to the way
she speaks to you.

Listen to the people
she uses

to touch your soul.

To touch your heart.
She's *always* with you.

Always listening.

Always guiding.
Always there.

Especially
during the moments

you think
you're all alone.

You're not.

And you never have been.
And you never
will be.

Take it all in.
She has so much love
for you.

Inhale it deeply.

Every message
she gives you.

Is yours
for the taking.

"Maybe I am.

*You know the universe
has a funny way*

*of communicating
with others.*

*With those
who need it most.*

Sometimes
it uses random people
to translate a message

to those who need it.

It's a blessing
in disguise," I replied.

"Maybe I
just . . . Am."

WHEN YOU FOLLOW YOUR HEART, THINGS BEGIN TO BLOOM, AND THINGS BEGIN TO SPEAK TO YOU IN WAYS YOU NEVER IMAGINED

"She left, bro.

Something bad
happened to her,

and she didn't even care
to tell me

why she left.

Not until six months after
or so.

And now
it has been

about two years
of a painful

long-distance
relationship.

And almost every night
I feel
like shit."

Now distance
is a funny little thing.

It can make you
or break you.

It can make the relationship stronger
or

dismantle it.

Distance can go
either way.

It is a test
of your commitment.

A test
of your heart's heart.

*"Why were you
in a long-distance relationship*

to begin with?" I asked.

"School? Work? Family?"

"Her dad," he said.

"Her dad?"

*"He passed away
last June.*

*And she left
to be with him*

*right before
he passed,*

to care for him.

*Which I completely
understand.*

*But she never came back.
She stayed.*

*I don't know
what this means.*

*It's been two years
since it happened, too."*

*"What's holding you back
from going*

with her?" I asked.

"Nothing."

*"Well,
maybe you should*

consider it.

*I don't need
to know the details.*

*But if you love her
and she loves you,*

then

*I think you should
make the move*

and be with her.

You have to understand
that she lost

her father.

And she is probably
out there

keeping her mother's
spirits high.

As things usually
fall apart

when someone passes on," I said.

"And I know
this distance is probably

eating you alive.

And I'm sure
you have your own

obligations at home.
But I want you

to understand

that if she is the one,
then she should be

your first priority," I added.

"I also think
if you want

to be with her,

then you should.

If you want
to be with her,

make that transition.

I believe
the only thing stopping you

is yourself."
"Yeah . . ." he said.

"Besides,
will you ever meet

a girl like her?

Ask yourself that,
then follow your heart.

I said
follow your heart.

And follow your heart
again.

There is no better way
to live.

No better way
to love."

Imagine that.
How beautiful

it
can all be . . .

if only
we all

followed . . .
our hearts.

WHEN EVERYONE ON THE PLANET IS AN ASSHOLE, DOES THIS MAKE YOU ONE, AS WELL?

The music was low.
The bartender was running

her shifts.

The lights were dimmed.
And the crowd

was light.

I could feel
my best friend's sadness

radiating
like beams

shooting out of her pores.

"I had a deep connection with him," she said.

*"But he was no
good to me.*

*He was always angry.
Too sensitive . . .
everything pissed him off."*

"Yeah," I said.

*"Like it got
to the point*

*where anything I said
would bother him.*

*Every little thing
would piss him off.*

*And he made me feel
like shit*

most of the time."

*"Was it always
like this?*

*I don't remember
how it was*

in the beginning," I said.

*"No.
Not at all.*

He was different.

Kinder.
Sweeter.

More attentive.

I would say
the first six months
were bliss."

She went on.

She had so much
on her chest.

I was beginning to wonder
how she could move

with all of that
weight

trapped in her body.
All of that pain.

It was as if
she had an entire

mountain
on her back

and she was walking across

the hottest dessert
during

the hottest day
of the summer.

I felt bad for her.

She was my friend.
I had known her

all my life.

And we had been
good friends

through the best
and worst

of times.

*"I'm just so
broken right now,"* she said

as she took a drink
off her sour-apple martini.

*"I think maybe
he was an asshole*

*before you met him
and during.*

*And he'll be one
long after this."*

She started to laugh.

*"You always say
the darndest things.*

*But you're right.
He is an asshole."*

"I'm kidding.
I think a lot of people

do that
in the beginning.

I think a lot of people
don't let

their true colors show
because they're afraid

someone might
not like them.

We're all just looking
for someone

to hold
in the end, you know?

But in a lot of ways,
once they get

too comfortable
and know they have you,

they start being
careless

with what they say
and do with you.

People are like that,
you know?

We have all
done this

at some point.

That's why I said

maybe he was just
an asshole

long before he met you.

Who knows
what type of relationships
he had before you.

Who knows
how fucked-up

his childhood was, etc.

You know a lot of people
carry

a lot of pain,
and they're afraid

to speak about it.

And they lash out
their pain

on those who
care the most.

That's the way it is
sometimes," I said.

"Yeah . . . I get it."
"But still . . .
he is an asshole.

A giant one."

She began to lightly laugh again.

*"We just have to accept
the fact*

that we are lovers.

*And we are attracted
to assholes,"* I said.

She began to laugh
a little more.

*"That's just
the way things are,*

my love.

*That's just
the way*

we love."

I grabbed my beer
and raised it

and guzzled it down

to the last drop.

"And amen to that," I said.
"Amen," she replied.

WHEN I WAS A BOY, I MET A GIRL, AND THAT GIRL WAS SUPPOSED TO BE WITH ME FOREVER

I was madly
in love with you.

And that's not something
I'm afraid

to say.

That's not something
I keep

buried in the back
of my throat.

I loved you.

I really did.
And I really wanted
us

to work.

I really wanted
us
to last.

To be together forever.

That was something
we used to say

to each other.

I really wanted
us

to look past
all of the pain

we caused.

To maybe
move forward from the things
that hurt.

From the things
that led us
toward our doom.

I was
madly in love with you.

I really was.

More than anything
I had ever felt.

More than I
could ever imagine.

And I never thought
I would feel this way

about anyone.

And I wasn't
anticipating it,

either.

But then
you happened.

And you came into my life
like a flash.
Like a comet

in the sky.

Roaring through my darkness
to brighten up

my life.

And it was perfect
for a little while.

It was too good
to be true.

And I love you

for that.
For those memories.

I really appreciate them,
looking back.

And now
it's been
a really long time.
The memory of us

has become

something like a dream.

Something
so faded

that I question
some of these memories.

Did they really happen?

Are any of these
real

or not?

It's sad to say
it's been that long,

to the point
where I am confused

whether it be
fact or fiction.

But nonetheless,

I was
madly in love with you.

That is something
that demands

no questioning.

I did
love you.

Fully
and without regret.

And I just wanted us
to work.

But sadly,
it didn't.

And now
all that is left

is distortion.
A white noise
of you.

A space
in my heart

that I can't
make out,

but I know
deep down inside

it represents
you.

WHEN A REAL FRIEND FINDS YOU, THEY REALLY NEVER EVER KNOW HOW TO LET YOU GO

I was sitting
in a bar

with my longtime
childhood friend, Daisy.

We were catching up
after a few years

of not
seeing each other.

She looked great.

Same smile.
Same eyes.

Same soul.

But she did seem
a bit off

the whole time.
She kept looking
at her phone.

It was almost
as if

she was expecting
someone

to text or call her.

Not like I was keeping track,
but she was glued

to it

every fifteen minutes,
I would say.

It was a bit
distracting.

And then
in the midst of it all,

she spewed
what was on her mind.

Or at least
what I thought

was on her mind
the whole time.

*"It's just
sometimes*

*I don't know
how to let go.*

*I don't know
when to start*

or end things.

*I have no control
over what I feel.*

*I feel so lost
sometimes,"* she said.

It took a second
for me to gather my thoughts.

After all,
it had been such a long time

since I'd seen her.

I kind of lost
my train of thought

looking at her lips
and eyebrows.

It was one of those things
I couldn't

get my eyes off.

*"You will end up
where you belong.*

*So don't worry
too much*

*about what
you're going through.
Learn from it.
but don't dwell on it.*

Feel it
and then . . .

let go.

What's yours
will find you.

No matter what happens.

Everything you deserve
will come to you.

It will manifest.

You'll see.
Whether it be love.

Personal growth.
Knowledge.

Friendship.
Moving on.
Healing . . . etc.

Whatever it may be.

It will come to you.
And it will find you.

And stay with you.
No matter what," I replied.

"You really think so?" she asked
as she smiled.

"Yes. I really do," I said.

And just like that,

the music in the bar
seemed a little smoother.

And her soul
felt a little calmer.

And her heart
seemed

a little brighter.

Sometimes
a few words

are what you need
to get you going.

Sometimes
that's all it takes.

A few words
from someone you trust.

Someone you've known.
And someone

you love.

THINGS ALWAYS SEEMED A LITTLE BETTER WHEN WE WERE YOUNGER, BUT IT ONLY MEANT WE HAD A GREAT TIME GROWING UP

"You can't run away
from all of your problems.

Sometimes

you have to face them.
Face your fears.

Face your hardest
challenges.

Face . . .
what hurts.

You can't hide
forever.

You can't let
these things

control your feelings.

Your emotions.
Your decisions.

Sometimes
you have to fight.

Sometimes
you have to stand up

against
what's holding you back.

What's holding you
down.

You were meant
to fly, baby.

Meant
to spread your wings

and soar.

And not worry
about looking back.

Or looking down.

This is your life.
Take it back.

Do
what makes you happy.

Regardless
of the obstacles ahead.

You got this.
I know you do," I said

to my friend Julie
one starry night

under the stars.

We used to hang out
with a group of friends

in the middle
of *SOUTH BEACH*

with some beers, wine,
and weed.

Those were indeed
the good times.

"But it's so hard.

So hard to begin.
So hard to change.

To follow
your dreams.

I just don't know," she said.

"No one does,
my love.

No one knows
how to begin.

How to change.
How to follow
one's dreams.

This is not
something we know.

It's just
something we do.

Little by little.

Day by day.
And when you look back,

you realize
how much

has really changed.

But it all
starts now.

By doing the little things
that speak to you.

By doing
the things you feel
are for you.

Little by little.
Day by day.
By choosing yourself
over the people

who hurt you.

By learning the difference
between

who actually cares
and who doesn't.

And it's not something
you will pick up

overnight.

But with time,

you will learn.
You will.

Just don't be
so hard on yourself.

This is your life.

*And you're allowed
to make mistakes.*

*As long as you learn
from them.*

*And as long
as you follow*

*what makes you feel
at home."*

*"Thank you, Bobby . . .
you really are*

a special friend." she said.

*"You are welcome
And . . .*

I know."

WHEN THE WINDOWS OF YOUR SOUL ARE BROKEN, THE FAINTEST WIND STILL MAKES A SOUND . . . STILL MAKES AN IMPACT

No matter who you are,

I hope
you know

that in the times
you are lonely,

in the times
you feel broken

and beaten
to the ground,

know

that you are someone.

That you are
important.

That you are
just as special

and as rare
and as beautiful

as everyone else.
Know

that things
will get better.

And know
that life is not meant

to be easy.

That it is meant
to put you through

the harshest things.

No matter who you are,
know your place.

Know your significance.

You are loved.
You are needed.

Know this.

Especially in
your darkest of times.

WHEN WHAT YOU KNOW IS NOT WHAT YOU WANT, BUT IT IS WHAT YOU NEED

When the world seems
to have given up

on you,

know
that it is not over.

Know
that you are not

defined
by them.

By those who want
to hurt you.

By those who say
they love you

but show you
no love.

Know
that you

and only you
know who you are.

That you
and only you

know what you are
capable of.

When the world seems
to have given up

on you,

know
that it is not over.

That sometimes the world
will not

understand you.
That sometimes this
will lead

toward disappointment.

Toward pain.

Toward suffering.
That knowing this

will sometimes
make you feel alone.

When the world seems
to have given up

on you,

know
that you are not

the only one
who feels this way.

That many of us
deal with this type
of feeling.
That many of us

feel

as if there is no one
out there

for us.

To guide us.
To help us.
To save us.

To talk to us.
To understand us.

Know
that you are never

truly
alone in this.

Someone has been there before.

When the world seems
to have given up

on you,

know
that it is not over.

Know
that tomorrow is a new day.

Rain or shine.

Pain or laughter.
Know

that you will always

have
a second chance.

At love.
At finding a new job.

At working on yourself.
At wanting more.

At finding

something new
about yourself.

And working on those things
that bring you down.

When the world seems
to have given up

on you,

know
that it is not over.

That it is completely normal
to feel this way

sometimes.

That it is okay
to isolate yourself

for a while.

That it is okay to reflect.
To recollect.

To face what it is
that hurts you

or even
to do nothing.

Know
that the choice is yours.

That it is always
yours.

No matter what.

When the world seems
to have given up

on you.

Know
that it is not over.

Know
that you were built

for this.
That you can pull through.
And every journey

will make you stronger.

Wiser.
More understanding of things.

Of yourself

and of how you deal
with things.

Know this.

When the world seems
to have given up

on you.

Know
that it is not over.

Know
that it is okay

to have regrets.

That it is okay
to take a loss.

To make
a bad decision.

To feel lost
every once in a while.

Know
that this is okay

and it is
a part of your life.

To have doubt.

To have fear.
And to not be so sure

of your future.

Know
that this is how
it works.

That this is how the world is.
And it's okay.

Know
that you are okay.

And that you
will be okay.

No matter what happens.

So when the world seems
to have given up

on you.

Know
that it must

give up on you
sometimes . . .
in order to make
you know.

To make you feel.

To confirm.
To reassure.

Over and over again.

That you are significant.
That you are beautiful.

In your flaws
and all.

Know this
and remember this

during times
of extreme regret.

During times
of pain.

Of loneliness.
Of sadness, etc.

Know your place
in the world.

Know your importance.
And stand.

And breathe.

And know with all your heart,
whatever it is

you are seeking
will come to you

when you need it
most.

WHEN YOU WAKE UP IN THE MIDDLE OF THE NIGHT AND REALIZE YOU HAVE WINGS

You let go
when you want to.

When you are ready.

No matter how many times
you tell yourself.

Or how many times
you try to convince

yourself
you are over it.

If you're not,
then you are not.

You only truly let go
when it no longer

affects you.

When it no longer
crawls beneath
your skin.

You only really let go
when you are ready.

And when you are willing
to set

yourself free.

WHEN YOU FUCK WITH HER HEART . . . IT CAN ALL BACKFIRE . . . IT CAN BRING YOU THE TYPE OF PAIN THAT NEVER REALLY BURNS AWAY

"I know
you're doing your best,

and I'm proud
of you," I said

as the music
in the background played.

"It's just hard.

I'm trying so hard
to move on.

But I can't.

Everywhere I go.
Everything I see.

Every moment.
Every second.

With friends.
And even when I'm
all alone.

*All I think about
is her.*

*And the way I fucked
it all up."*

I knew it was his fault.

When it was all
said and done,

it was *really* him.

He would put her last.
He wouldn't put in

the time
she needed to bloom.

The time
they needed

for their relationship to grow.
I knew
it was him.

But it was just
very hard to tell him that.

Especially
while he was breaking apart

right
before my eyes.

*"And now
look at me,"* he said

as he unlocked his phone
and turned off

the music playing from it.

*"I'm a mess now.
And I wish*

I could take it all back."

For a moment.
Time stood still.
And I felt

for reasons unknown
as if

now was the right moment.

And I was the right person
to tell him

the truth.

"The thing is,
you took her for granted.

You probably thought
she would never

leave you, either.

But you can't rely
on history

to make a relationship last.
You can't rely
on what you've been through.
She's human.

She needs love.
She needs gentleness.

She needs attention.

That emotional
and spiritual bond.

And I know you fucked up.

I would see it
every time

I hung out with the both
of you.

You would embarrass her
to make a joke.

You would demand her
to go get you things

when your buddies were around.
And sometimes
you would raise your voice."

"I know," he said as he shrugged.

"And that's
just what I saw, man.

I don't know
what really went on.

But that's not the way
you treat someone

you love.

Someone
you want to keep.

She's gone now.
And she isn't coming back.

But that doesn't mean
you can't better prepare yourself

for your next
relationship.

That doesn't mean
you can't grow

and learn from this experience.

Take this brokenness.

Learn from it.
And never forget this pain

you're feeling.

There is good
in this moment.

Although
it is very hard

to see it.

But there is.

You will take everything
from this
experience
and make sure you don't
pass it to the next."

"I know.
But right now

I'm just so fucked-up," he said.

"I know.
But this is how

you become a man.

This is how
you become a better person.

Take this moment.

And take it in slowly.
Better days are ahead

of you.

The sun will shine
upon you again, my friend.

Just don't go ahead
and fuck around

with girls' hearts."

WHEN YOUR FEAR CONTROLS YOUR HEART, THEN EVERYTHING YOU DO IS OUT OF LINE

You think
you are not

good enough.

But the reality is,
you are.

You are everything
and more.

Don't let your doubts
bury your light.

Don't let your fear
control

what you're meant to feel.
You are enough.

And please
stop comparing yourself
to everyone

you know.

We all have
our own journey.

Our own calling.

Just be patient
with yourself.

Everything soon
will make sense.

I promise.

r.h. Sin

She just stood there, tired beneath a restless sky,
few stars in sight, the moon full of glow. It had
been raining all afternoon, evident by how her
bare feet made tracks on the soft ground—gazing
upon the ocean, casting her inner light against the
horizon like a beautiful lighthouse searching for
something more. The disappointment was written
continuously on pages of her soul, yet she clung
to hope as the waves reached for the shore. She's
done this often; waiting has become a part of her
life. And sadly, her heart longs for a love that
appears to be shipwrecked, lost at sea, lifeless at
the bottom of everything she can see.

Those beautiful, sad eyes, searching for
something to calm the storm. Fingers waiting to
grasp what deserves to be touched, lips readily
willing to speak the truth of love to the ears of her
beloved. But that isn't it now, and this dream is so
far away that it's beginning to fade. What is love
but a fantasy to someone who has only seen it
with closed eyes? What is true love for someone
who has only kissed the lips of a liar? And why
does true love hide primarily from the heart
willing to receive it and provide it in abundance?
These are the answers she searches for while
staring into the depths of the night, awaiting a
mate for her soul.

It begins the way you wish it would, a dream
coming true, a flower deciding to blossom despite
the cold. You question it, but only for a moment,
then you're off and away, lifted by your feelings
of love. You accept what stands before you,
allowing that person into places still destroyed by
the last fire that burned your heart. You tell them
everything, your hopes and dreams; you even
share with them your fears and all the things that
broke your heart before they walked into your
life. While it has been difficult to trust others,
you slowly let your guard down because their
consistency chips away at the wall you built in
front of your heart. You think to yourself, "I can
finally be happy."

Remember?

And now, all that's left is a memory of a love
that faded with time. All that remains are lies,
an unfortunate truth. A dream that removed its
mask to reveal a waking nightmare. The sad thing
about a tragedy is that the beginning doesn't feel
like one. There is hope and potential, and there is
calm and safe, but in the end, you see it for what
it was meant to be. A beautiful feeling that leads
to chaos and yet another dead end. You're back
where you started, stronger but afraid. Deserving
of love but weary from trying to find it.

Telling a woman she's the one but "not right now" is emotional abuse.

i didn't mind the sadness

the pain within me

just meant that my heart

had awakened

to the truth of what

you made me feel

and while this hurts

i'm grateful

for this realization

————————

i have cried more than April

i've been colder than December

each year always changing

and by the end, it's always the same

————————————

sadness is more reliable than joy

happiness is eager to leave

but heartache has always

fought to stay

she is a master at sadness
a Queen sitting on a throne
made of despair

a walking tragedy
fighting to find
the time to be happy

she desires something
she can't find

she's in love with someone
who won't give her what
she needs

she's alone beside a lover
who hates to see her smile

she'd rather be laughing
but she's crying right now

you keep staring

at the clock

you see your value

in the numbers

but you don't realize

that you are timeless

———————————

it's incredibly sad
to think
that the boat we built
was always bound
to sink

the love we shared
was doomed to perish
once swelled with feeling
now rendered careless

the sadness

this pain

will make one hell

of a story

told from the lips

of a survivor

_____

sadly

we hurt others

all in an effort

to cure our own pain

but you will never

leave hell

setting fire

to someone's heart

a grudge is a chain

connecting you

to everything

you should have

left behind

the painful thing about betrayal
is that it doesn't stop the heart
from loving the one
who deceived you

and the tragedy of it all
is knowing that you must move on
despite everything within you
begging to stay

your mind at war
with your heart
on a battlefield
in opposition
to the one
you believed
would protect you

_____

staying with someone
because you don't want
to hurt them

destroys their chances
of being with someone
who loves them without doubt

_____

i am good at being abandoned

i am a genius in heartbreak

the only love i know is fleeting

all the promises are empty

and forever is all a lie

————————————

you thought

you'd left your heart

in the hands of your abuser

but the pain you feel in your chest

just lets you know

that your heart is still yours

———————

one day, i'll leave you

like you left me

one day, i'll learn

to stop remembering

the things

you easily forgot

_____

my memory of you

is a ghost

that still haunts me

———————

it's hard to be present

when everything

you've loved

has been left behind

fading slowly

beneath the weight of time

—————————

waiting for you to change

is like trying to grow a garden

in the desert in June

the worst wounds

are the ones

trapped in darkness

beneath the skin

beside the heart

inside the mind

———————

you were taught

to stay clear of strangers

but most of the pain

and trauma in your life

have been caused

by the people you know

you were taught

to protect yourself

against unseen forces

but as you look into the eyes

of your attacker

you see a familiar face

thrown overboard
and left at sea
i begged the devil
to set me free

with loss of hope
i try to wait
i asked the moon
to keep me safe

the night is vast
try not to drown
these waves of sadness
push me down

the void of night
still here, i float
i think you'll come
but i know you won't

_____

it was never heaven
you chose this hell

it was never love
the hate was hidden

the person you knew
has never existed

stop giving real feelings
to a fraudulent person

_____

my mind

crowded

by what you promised

my heart

broken

by lies and betrayal

my soul

weary

from all the searching

———————

each lie

a shard of glass

i feel you

pricking

at my skin

———————————

the years

you spent

being loyal

were the years

they were not

_____

what is love

but a bird

sitting for a moment

flying away in an instant

refusing to stay

difficult to capture

singing a song

a beautiful melody

fading into the wind

always moving on

above our heads

out of reach

————————

"it could have been different"
is the lie you dance with

holding the hands of a ghost
haunted by an illusion

and here i was

adding flames

to my hell

the longer i resisted

ending things with you

most of what
you've lost
were the things
you believed
you'd always keep

your past, filled with
all the lies
that first sounded
like melodies of love

and even as your feet
plant themselves in this moment
you're stuck, longing for something
that was never really what you
expected it to be in the first place

move on, please . . .

_____

it is never in what they say

the truth tells itself in their actions

you struggle to see past the bullshit

the words become beautiful distractions

and so it feels
like the sun
has been in a rush
to leave me

the darkness arrives
before i can prepare for it
the light i long for
the moon can't deliver

these shades of gray
are reflective of my suffering
the hum of the wind
matches the sound of my heart

the days are shorter than usual
the warmth no longer lingers
a chill in the air
my heart has run cold

_____

searching for peace

inside of the hearts

of those who

constantly let you down

is a chaotic thing to do

i'm tired from all the nights

of fighting to be braver

and stronger than

i actually feel

―――――――――

you are my secret sorrow

the thing i never talk about

the hurt that i hide

with laughter

_____

sometimes the opposite

of sadness is not joy

on those cold nights

you realize that sometimes

that alternative to pain

is simply feeling nothing

When there is no love in the center of those four walls, your home becomes a prison. This was true for her, standing by herself at the window of her 22nd-floor apartment, watching the lovers pass by on foot, hand in hand, overwhelmed with feelings she'd come to believe were nonexistent. For so much of her life, the genuine joy that emanated from a loving relationship had been out of her reach. Not for nothing, she'd tried several times to fall in love and one too many times with a counterpart who wasn't willing to fall beside her. So when she observed the couples, nearly floating off the ground as they walked, filled with excitement, she watched in wonder, and for those few seconds, she'd attempted to dream herself into their shoes without success. Even the rain was a symbolic gesture toward understanding what storms lay awake in her chest, but the strange thing was, the rain seemed to become a playground for those in love as their laughter echoed at a similar volume as their feet, stepping in and out of puddles.

Genuine love can't exist in the expressions of the fraudulent, and many liars have crossed the intersection of her heart, but there is something inside her that still believes. That sort of hopefulness, despite all the heartbreak, is beautiful despair.

_____

all my energy spent
tired and rainy nights
days when the sun
does not care to reach me

cornered by guilt and shame
overwhelmed with regret
searching for love
where it'll never exist

staring into a mirror
confronting someone
who has never known love
face-to-face with my only friend

_____

the heaviness of being betrayed

hits you the hardest at night

_____

when trust begins to shatter
the apologies and the promises
begin to lose all meaning

_____

when you're tired this way

sleeping is so fucking hard to do

for once

i'd love to know

the feeling of bliss

that comes with

the realization

that the person i love

is happy to have me

in their life

———————————

i've tried shutting my mind off

the more i think

the more i break

———————

so often

you are stressed

by someone

who doesn't even care

if you're okay

_____

and so it seems

forever is meant for sadness

and not for love

———————————

you've been waiting for someone
who has been pursuing someone else
always waiting to be loved
by the person who overlooks you

expecting to be seen by someone
who will never comprehend
the meaning of your love
or the power in your presence

_____

alone in a glass cube

overlooking the city

you hide your sadness

from the world

but i've seen you

dreary eyed

keeping secrets

that break you

_____

maybe the city that never sleeps

sits wide awake with thoughts of loneliness

the city, made to appear exciting

but, in truth, this Apple is empty

_____

The worst type of people are the ones who will accuse you of doing things to them that they've been doing to you in secret.

and so

it seems

the moon

hid itself

from me

the midnight sky

a ghoulish gray

the darkness dwells

it starts to rain

the sadness lives

forever more

no knob in sight

a secret door

my heart

it breaks

in pieces now

my weary eyes

below my brow

_____

you come last to their friends

and second to their phone

you don't exist on their social media

you're the thing that no one sees

and they rarely make time

and they barely tell the truth

they're not concerned about your mind

don't give a fuck about your peace

————————

This is pure torture, the way you confide in someone who isn't listening. Your attempt to fight for love has always been a lonely war. It's just you and your feelings, always giving, yet to receive. Falling to no end, your expectations are never met. Regret is something you struggle with, but you'd rather play pretend.

——————

It's wild how you actually think you can trust a
person who left someone for you.

Okay, here's the truth . . . in most cases, a man only wants to maintain a "friendship" with you after a breakup to maintain some sort of control over you and to stand in the way of any chance of you being fully committed and happy with someone who isn't them. It's not a real friendship; he's just pocketing you in case he wants to double back, and if he feels he's found someone who he feels can replace you fully, he'll eventually abandon you.

———————————

A man who doesn't openly speak you into his
future doesn't plan to have you in it.

———————

you're not even friends
with your friends
your family speaks to you
like some stranger off the street

the person you love
makes you hate the fact
that you love them
and that sadness
has brought you here
to me

the distance between

anger and sadness

is so short

_____

she's sitting on the line

between giving up

and waiting to see

if things will change

_____

when you're dating

a narcissist

you apologize

even when

you've done

nothing wrong

———————

you destroyed me beautifully

telling me all the things

i longed to hear

perfect, empty lies

meaningless but profound

———————

you miss me

but you never stay

_____

maybe they changed; maybe you never knew them
to begin with

maybe what you loved about them was their ability

to pretend to be the very thing you dreamed of

maybe it hurts this bad because you've been alone

for far too long

_____

the person you explained

in detail about what broke

your heart in the past

will still break you

in the same way

despite knowing

how much damage

it'll cause

and it hurts to read this

because this has happened

to you

_____

you overthink

and overlove

the most

underwhelming people

———————————

what the fuck is wrong with you
haven't i been good to you
saw distance and destroyed
the lines between us
moved mountains, demolished hills
walked through rain, sleet, and snow
as if it were the summer sun

treated it like a breeze
but it was the eye of a hurricane
and still, i fought it, running toward you
unafraid where others would be afraid
and, somehow, you say
that i've not done enough
what the fuck

blisters on my hands
from holding on too tight
rusty nails beneath my feet
despite that, i'm running
in your direction
even though i should be
running away from you

———————————

what to do with the pain

when you've run out of tears

and excuses to tell yourself

what to do with the heartbreak

when it's too deep

unreachable by kind gestures and hope

what is tomorrow

when you can't get through today

what is true love

when all it's ever been was a lie

—————————

even the most confident soul

can be forced to question itself

loving the wrong person

fills good people with doubt

even the strongest of us all

can struggle to get out

even those most worthy

of truth are lied to

you are the most beautiful thing

and i'm sorry about

all the love they denied you

_____

that desire to open up

that urge to let your guard down

but the person you want

to be vulnerable with

continues to give you reasons

as to why you should remain guarded

that feeling itself

is painfully draining

_____

you knew it would destroy me

you planned it all out

you even imagined the way

i'd respond when it was done

but none of that stopped you

_____

there are days when you

feel like certainty

and others

when you are my oblivion

_____

your heart has been broken

more times than it's been loved

_____

you're restless

because sleep

requires the type of peace

you no longer know

_____

i wanted to build

my world around you

but all this time

you were Armageddon

I'm convinced that we listen to music so loud to silence the demons whispering in our hearts.

To the reader, to the one with a broken heart
reading these words in the middle of the night,
I hope you know that you are more than the
heartache; you are more than what has been done
to you.

———————

the people

who make you feel

like an inconvenience

do not deserve

to be made a priority

in your life

———————

i'm tired of being almost happy

i'm weary from being almost loved

_____

i wonder where i lost myself

sometimes i wish i could go back

to be the person you loved

———————————

That's what hurts the most. You're constantly asking if everything is okay between you both, and they say yes, even while they're thinking about your replacement.

_____

Pure evil, the people who cheat on you while promising you that there is no one else.

year by year

the distance grows

we carry on

as if we don't know

———————

holding you
felt empty
you are here
and still
somewhere else

―――――――――――

to the girl
whose father
abandoned her

to the girl whose mother
displayed moments of jealousy

to the girl whose siblings
judged her for being different

feeling as if you don't belong
in your own home
looking into the eyes
of your family
and seeing strangers

you are worthy
you are intelligent
you are strong
you are beautiful
you are you
and that is enough

_____

it hurts to wake up

in your own body

and no longer know

who you are

it hurts to see a stranger

in your reflection

They tell you to use your words to express the
way you feel to the person who has made you
feel those things, but what they fail to say to you
is that those words have no meaning and carry no
weight when spoken to a person who no longer
sees the need to consider the way they make you
feel. It's frustrating, really; you speak calmly, soft
in your approach. Seeking out some sign of hope,
longing for compassion, and being left confused
by the cold response from a person you believed
had your best interest. Nothing changes, because
they disregard everything you tell them; they
have no interest in being held accountable, as the
need to make you feel heard or seen is just not
a priority.

––––––––––––––––

It fell apart so fucking easily because you tried to
hold it together with lies.

Small secrets become big lies.

————————

You feel unwanted, so you get distant.

————————————

That shit is sick. The way they get angry about
being accused of something they're actually
doing behind your back.

A person can love you and not like you.

_____

It's exhausting as fuck being the one to initiate every act of kindness in a relationship.

_____

Cheaters are so obsessed with being with loyal
people. It's psychotic.

_____

Your demeanor for most things is rigid, cold, and resentful. I'm not bothered by what you say; it's the energy you push toward me. It has become so apparent that what I've been feeling over time is that you don't actually like me, and as that resentment has grown, the tougher things are, the harder things get. That's the energy you give me, and that's the way you make me feel; whether you care or not, this is the truth, my truth.

———————————

Your voice changes whenever you speak to
anyone outside of me; it's like you come to life
for strangers, like you sort of died on me. Pretend
that I'm the worst; it's like you like to lie on me.
I've been the one to put you first; recently, I'm
last to be. Oblivious to my heartache, one day
you'll see the last of me. All I wanted was your
love, but you would rather be mad at me.

It's always raining here, inside my heart, and
I'm left searching for an umbrella I never bought
because you promised me that there would always
be sunshine. The lies are so pretty. I tried to build
our relationship on a bunch of half-truths and
empty promises, not knowing it at the time. And
no relationship is perfect; that's been the excuse I
give whenever I'm alone with the thought of how
much this hurts. I don't open up to anyone, afraid
that I'd be betraying your trust, but the truth is,
I'm fully aware that you show no concern for the
way I believe in you. Constantly doing things to
break my heart, continuously making choices that
dissolve what trust I have left in this.

It's always raining here, and yet here I am,
beneath a storm for you. Beneath a black cloud,
standing above fragile ground. Alone to face it all,
back against a wall, cornered by endless amounts
of regrets and unanswered questions. My feet
tired from pacing back and forth to the exit, my
knees weary from supporting the weight that you
left on my shoulders.

Why was it never good, "it" being the effort, the
time? The endless energy forced into an empty
corner of your heart with hopes of taking up
residence there, but still there was no room for
me. Wanting desperately to build a future with
you, but there is no room for us. Damaged, left in
ruins by a flood of neglect and your unwillingness
to protect. It's always raining here, and I'm tired
of getting wet.

r.h. Sin index

Beautiful Sad Eyes, Weary Waiting for Love copyright © 2023 by r. h. Sin and Robert M. Drake. All rights reserved. Printed in China. No part of this book may be used or reproduced in any manner whatsoever without written permission except in the case of reprints in the context of reviews.

Andrews McMeel Publishing
a division of Andrews McMeel Universal
1130 Walnut Street, Kansas City, Missouri 64106

www.andrewsmcmeel.com

23 24 25 26 27 SDB 10 9 8 7 6 5 4 3 2 1

ISBN: 978-1-5248-8506-9

Library of Congress Control Number: 2023933576

Editor: Patty Rice
Art Director: Diane Marsh
Production Editor: Elizabeth A. Garcia
Production Manager: Julie Skalla

ATTENTION: SCHOOLS AND BUSINESSES
Andrews McMeel books are available at quantity discounts with bulk purchase for educational, business, or sales promotional use. For information, please e-mail the Andrews McMeel Publishing Special Sales Department: sales@amuniversal.com.

W0009424

WEARY WAITING FOR LOVE

r. h. Sin

WEARY WAITING FOR LOVE

Robert M. Drake

Andrews McMeel
PUBLISHING®

ROBERT M. DRAKE
contents

ROBERT M. DRAKE

WHEN YOUR BEST IS NOT ENOUGH, KNOW THAT SOMEWHERE IN THAT HURTING BODY THERE IS MORE

You will hurt
when you are meant

to hurt.

And love
when you are meant

to love.

No matter how good
you are

to people.

No matter what
you do
or don't do.

Whatever it may be.

If it's meant for you,

then
it is meant for you.

Whether it be sadness
or happiness.

What's yours
will find you.

And it will show you
what you need

to know.

What you need
to experience

in order for you
to grow.

And at the right time, too.

Like I said,
what is meant for you

is meant
for you.

And no one can take
that away.

No one can dictate
what is going on

in your life
right now

at this
very instant.

Just know . . .
how it is exactly

where you need
to be.

So take these experiences
as they come.

Take them in
with all heart.

With all soul.

And
at your own pace.

There are lessons
to be learned

from everything.

Bad or good.
Lessons to be

passed down,
despite your best efforts

to avoid them.

WHEN SOMEONE ELSE'S PAIN CONNECTS SOMEWHERE IN YOUR HEART ... YOU BECOME THEM ... YOU BECOME MORE

*"I couldn't delete
my grandfather's number*

when he died," she said.

*"I just couldn't.
And sometimes I read*

*the last message
he wrote me."*

*"I have the same problem
with people,"* I said.

*"It's hard for me
to let go*

*when I know
they're no longer*

with me.

*But I'm curious,
what was
the last message*

he said to you?" I asked.

There was a small pause
between us.

It snuck onto us
like a mouse

crossing an alleyway.

It came.
And it went.

And then she took
a deep breath,

as if
what she was about to say

was meant
to change my life.

He said, *"Be brave."*
"That was it?" I asked.

"'Be brave . . .

When the times
get hard.

Be brave.

When the people you love
are not with you.

Be brave.

When you think
you don't have it

under control.

Be brave.
My sweet girl.'

"And that was it," she added.
I was speechless.

Be brave.

When anything is not
going your way.

Be brave.

And there's no better way
to explain it

other than that.

WHEN IT IS HARD TO LET GO, YOUR HANDS BECOME VINES MADE OUT OF STONE, AND EVERYTHING YOU CARE ABOUT GETS DRAGGED FOR THE REST OF YOUR LIFE

I care.

And maybe more
than I should.

And maybe
I show it to those

who don't
deserve it at all sometimes.

But I can't help it.

It's a part of me.
I can't just leave

someone behind.

Especially
if we have some kind

of history
together.

It's hard.

And I can't see myself
doing it so

suddenly.

I know some people
can do that.

Cut others off
and leave them behind

and not think twice
about it.

But not me.

Even if someone
fucks me over,

I still give them
the benefit

of the doubt.

I still give them
a chance to apologize.

To change.

Maybe I'm a sucker
for thinking this way.

But I want to believe
in the greater good.

Someone has to.

Someone has to give
all the second chances.

Someone
has to put the effort in,
you know?

I think a lot of people
give up

too quickly on others.

A lot of people
don't want to dedicate
the time

because maybe
they think it's too hard

to help someone.

Or do things
for someone that'll make

them feel
a little less alone.

I think
maybe that's the main problem.

*People give up
on people*

too easily.

Especially those
who've been let down

more than once.
It becomes a cycle.

A repetitive force.

And sometimes
it's hard to steer away from.

But that's where
people like me

come into play.

I care.
So I show them

how they are not
forgotten.

How there's still
hope.

How there's still
someone who is willing

to stay.

No matter
what they do.

Sometimes
they just need

to be reminded.

Sometimes
that's the only thing

to do.

I WILL ALWAYS REMEMBER AND NEVER FORGET, WHEN IT RAINS, IT POURS, AND WHEN IT POURS, MY SOUL GETS CLEANSED ... THANK YOU FOR THIS MOMENT

On a cloudy afternoon
in 2003,

I found myself
standing in the bus stop,

waiting
for the next bus

to arrive.

There was a good number
of people.

About seven of us,
I recall.

And we were all
worried about the weather.

It was about to rain,
and none of us

obviously
wanted to get wet.

"Shoot, it's sprinkling," I said out loud.

I, for one,
was on my way

to a job interview.

And I couldn't really
show up

drenched in water
like a sponge.

An older man heard
what I said.

*"You're worried
about the rain?"* he asked

as he kept looking down
at his newspaper.

*"Yeah,
I can't afford
to get wet right now."*

*"You worried about
a little rain?"* he asked again.

*"Yeah . . .
I have a job interview
in an hour,"* I replied.

I was beginning to think
that perhaps

he didn't hear me
the first time.

"Aren't you worried?"

"Nah," he said
as he flipped a page

of his newspaper.
*"If you stand
in the rain long enough,*

*you begin to think
how nothing*

really matters
but this moment.

You begin to realize
how sometimes

we let
these small trivial things

run our lives.

Take control of them.
Sometimes we need

to learn
how not

to overreact
over little things like this.

So you get wet a little.
No big deal.

So you miss the bus.
No big deal.

So you don't get that job.
No big deal.

You will always have
another chance.

Another day.

Another moment
to pursue anything

you're trying to pursue."

In a lot of ways,
I began to think

that maybe
he was right.

Maybe
I was overreacting.

I had been
most of my life,

over the little things, too.

*"Just go with the flow
and feel,"* he said.

And after all these years,

those words
stuck with me.

Ever since,
I have always tried

to take things
a little more lightly.

You know,
not take myself

too seriously.
I try to laugh
a little more.

I try to relax
a little more.

I try to take my time
with things

a little more.

All my life,
I had been living

with strict rules,
and if something

went the wrong way,

I'd literally
lose my shit.

"Just go with the flow and feel."

And I did just that.
And I am still going.

And I'm still feeling.

And every time
the rain falls, I remember.

Amen.

WHEN YOU MEET A GIRL AND SHE CHANGES YOUR LIFE FOREVER

"How much do you care
about me?" she asked.

"Enough to break
my own heart," I said.

"Enough to put
you first,

even
before myself."

WHEN YOU MEET THEM, YOU WILL KNOW, AND I HOPE YOU REMEMBER THIS MESSAGE, NO MATTER WHAT

There are actually
people

who just
don't give a fuck

about anyone.

Who manipulate
in order to try to get

what they want.

I will never
ever

understand why people choose
to be this way.

And you will never
understand it,

either.

Because we don't
have an ounce

of that nonsense

in our bodies.

But it does exist—they
do exist.

A sea full of assholes
waiting to fuck

people over.

Especially
the ones

with good hearts.

WHEN YOU THINK YOU KNOW WHAT IS BEST FOR THEM, BUT YOU FAIL TO RECOGNIZE WHAT IS GOOD FOR YOU

"I didn't say anything to her."

"Nothing at all?
Are you mad?

Then why are you
so upset you

broke up with her?" I asked.

"Because
a part of me

feels like
I set her free."

For a moment,
I understood

where he was going
with this.

I understood

That, with all things you love
and appreciate,

there comes a time
when you must

decide

what's good for them
and not

what's *best* for you.

There comes a time
when you must

put them first.

Especially
over yourself.

In a lot of ways
now, looking back,

it was all
beginning to make sense
to me.

"You know
I couldn't keep her

with me
forever.

I don't have anything
to offer her.

And honestly,
she deserves better.

Deserves more.

I know it hurt
the both of us.

But in the long run,
she will be fine.

She will go on
and finish college.

Probably find herself
a good internship.

Then a good job.

And then . . .
a good man.

And live a perfect
happy life.

Somewhere
in a good, perfect town

or city.

That's something
I don't want to hold her back from," he said

as he held back his tears.

I understood him.

But I also wondered
why he couldn't

be that man
for her.

Why he couldn't
give her

what he said
she deserved.

And that's one thing
I really can't understand

That if you love someone
that deeply,

you don't
let them go.

You work on yourself
to become

that man
she deserves.
You get up
every day
and face it.

Face yourself until
you get it all right.

You just don't
quit on yourself

like that.

If anything,
by doing so,

you are quitting
on her.

By not giving her
the chance

to help you
make things right.

Besides,

no one knows the future.
No one knows

if she would have ended up
better or worse.

But this
we all knew.

That he gave up on her
the moment

he let go.

And some may say
it was heroic.

Some may say
it was a valiant

thing to do.

But none of that matters.
He let go

of the woman
he loved

for a reality
that didn't exist.

And that
may possibly be

one of the saddest
things

in the world.

WHEN YOUR BEST FRIEND HAS THE RIGHT WORDS ... TRUST THEIR INTUITION THAT THEY SOMETIMES KNOW YOU MORE THAN YOU KNOW YOURSELF

Maggie
was on her way

to do some holiday shopping.

She had picked up
her best friend,

Carol,
five minutes before.

The car radio was off.

The windows were rolled up tightly,
and the AC

was on the lowest setting.

*"I mean,
what do you do*

*if you're not in love
anymore?*

If you wake up

every morning

and you just don't feel it
anymore?" Maggie asked

as her car came
to a complete halt

in a Sears parking lot.

"I've been telling you
what to do

for the longest time."

"I know. I know.
It's just not that easy.

I can't just
spit out what I'm really

feeling.

It's not that simple," said Maggie.

"I think
you should just tell him

how you feel.
I mean,

there is no easy way
of putting it.

Besides
maybe he'll appreciate it."

"Appreciate it?
Me breaking his heart?"

"No. No.

He'll appreciate your honesty.
That's all we have

in the end.
And believe me.

Five. Ten.
Maybe even twenty years

down the road,

*that's what he'll remember
the most.*

*The fact
that you were honest*

with him.

*And the fact
that you were brave enough*

*to confront
how you felt,"* said Carol.

"I know, but it's so hard."

*"I think
when the time is right,*

you'll do it."

*"How will I know
when to say it?"*

"You'll just feel it.
You'll just know.

And believe me,
the right words

will surface.

It's one of those things
that just happens.

One of those things
you can't plan."

EVERY DAY CAN BE A NEW YEAR—ALL YOU NEED TO HAVE ARE THE RIGHT PEOPLE BESIDE YOU

In the bathroom
of her friend's home

during
a New Year's Eve party,

Mark found
Renee in tears.

He immediately noticed
her sobbing

and opened the door.

"Ren, you all right?"

"Go away, please.
Don't see me like this.

I've had too much
to drink
tonight.
Just please, go away!"

Of course, Mark
did not turn away.

He was concerned.

She had already been
missing

for about half an hour.

And he had been asking
everyone

around the party
if they had seen her.

"Ren . . ." Marked sighed
as he kneeled

beside her on the floor.

"I feel like
my life

is a complete failure.

And I'm sick
of trying to fix

everyone's problems.
I'm just done!

I'm so tired of it all!"

There was a brief pause.
A silence so loud

it's echo
fluttered down

the deepest parts
of the street.

"I know
what you're going through.

And I know
you're a strong woman.

But you're exhausted.
You're tired

from all the bullshit

you've had
to deal with

this whole year.

But sometimes
a strong woman

needs a shoulder
to lean on.

Needs at least
one person

to help her get through
the hardships

of life.

Sometimes
a strong woman
needs
that kind of support.

No matter how many battles
she has won

or lost.

Sometimes
a strong woman

just needs someone
to be there for her," said Mark

as Renee began
to sob even more.

The tears
began to fall out of her

like a faucet
running water.

"Everything's
going to be all right.

Everything
will work itself out.

Besides,
a new year

is right around the corner.

A new you
with new goals.

New self-discoveries.

So much
to look forward to, sis."

"You think so?"

"I know so.
Now c'mon.

Let me help fix you up,
and let's go back

to the party," said Mark

as the countdown
to the new year began.

It was about five minutes away.

Sometimes
that's all you need.

A friend
with a certain kind of light.

A certain kind
of warmth.

Sometimes
a friend can save your life.

They can pull the darkness
out of you.

They can bring out
the sun

in a stormy day.
And they can do it
so effortlessly.
Without contradiction
or regret.

Without the heaviness
of the world

and its sadness.

Sometimes a friend
is meant

to save you.

And sometimes
they save you

and never ask for anything
in return.

WHEN YOU DISCOVER YOUR TRUE SELF, YOU ARE ALLOWED TO BECOME WHO YOU WANT TO BECOME AND CHANGE IF YOU MUST ... ALWAYS

You need to step
outside of your

comfort zone sometimes.

You need to break
free

from the walls
you build

around yourself.

From the limits
you set on yourself, too.

You need to push
yourself toward

new things.

Toward
new experiences.

You can't let fear
stop you

from discovering
who you're meant to be.

From discovering

new things
you can possibly

fall in love with.

You can't let others
tell you

what to do
or how you should

live your life.

And you can't let others
marginalize you,

either.

This is your life.
And you need to do things

for you.

Even if,
at first,

you are afraid
to do so.

This is your life,
you hear me?!?!

And yours only,
and only you

can decide
on what you want

to love.
On what you
want to chase.

On what you
want to work on
or pursue.

This is your life!!

And you're allowed
to change.

To transform.

To go back
to things

you once loved,
and you're allowed

to let go of them, too.

As long
as everything you do

is meaningful
to you.

You're allowed
to live your life.

Allowed
to make mistakes.

Allowed
to learn from them.

Allowed
to work on your flaws.

To love yourself,
no matter what.

This is your life.

Understand this
and you will never lose sight

of what's important.

You will remember
why
you're
still here.

AMEN!

WHEN THOSE SAD BEAUTIFUL EYES
YEARN FOR A BEAUTIFUL HEART

It hurts.

To have all
of this love inside of you

and have no one
to give it to.

WHEN YOU FEEL IT, YOU JUST KNOW, AND WHEN YOU KNOW, YOU WILL FEEL IT

There is no
definitive answer

on how
to love someone.

No rules.
No guides.
No real instructions.

It's one of those
things

you do.

One of those
things

you feel.

Like being in a dark room
your whole life

and then,
in an instant,

you feel a light switch
and turn it on.

You look around.

You breathe.
And for the first time

in your life,

you finally recognize
you're home.

You finally understand.

Somehow
everything you've ever felt

makes sense.

That's what
love feels like

sometimes.

Like opening your eyes
for the first time

and knowing
deep

within your soul
that you belong.

WHEN YOU THINK YOU ARE LOSING IT, BUT IN REALITY IT IS ALL COMING TOGETHER

You're not crazy.

You just feel
too much.

You think
too much.

And that's special.

You're unique
because you care

about every
possible outcome.

You want things
to go

as planned.

You want things
to be perfect.

To go your way.

But life
isn't always

like this,
as you know.

Life
is not fair.

Life
is not going to comfort you

when you need it
most.

The real world is cruel.

The real world
is cold.

Lonely.
Sad.
Painful.

And that's why
you need to learn

how to let things go.

How to let
things be.

Like this,
disappointment won't be so harsh

on you.

Like this,
you will learn how nothing

lasts forever.

Like this,
you will appreciate things

for what they are.

For how they arrive
and for how

they go.

But first,
you need stop *overthinking*.

Stop
overanalyzing everything,

because
you will drive yourself mad.

You can't control
everything.

You can't make people do
what you wish them to do.

You can't change
the past.

And you definitely
can't stop

what your heart wants.

But you can learn
how to control these feelings

that keep happening

within you.

Learn
how to keep them at bay.

Like this,
you will learn

how to breathe.

Learn
how to love.

And learn
how to live your best life.

That's all.

WHEN THE LOVE STORY OF YOUR LIFE IS A LIE, BUT SHORTLY AFTER YOU REALIZE YOUR WORTH

"He didn't deserve you," I said,

after a long
conversation with Summer,

one of my best
childhood friends.

"He just didn't."

She was sobbing over it.
Of course she was.

She had spent
over six years

trying to make things work.

And I wasn't sure
if she was crying

over the fact
she lost

that much time with him
or the fact

that,
perhaps,

she really believed in him
and was let down

to the point
of no return.

"It's just,
I gave so much of myself

to him.

So much
of my time.

My heart . . ."

she said, as she continued to sob.

Uncontrollably
at one point.

I, myself, wasn't even sure
of how to comfort her.

It was one of those moments
you just had

to ride out.

Let things sail.

Similar
to her relationship.

It was time
to let go.

To start over.

No matter how much love
she gave

or how much time
she lost.

It was time.
There was no other way

but
to move forward

and try to put the past behind her.

"You know . . .

*Sometimes things happen
for a reason.*

*Actually,
everything happens*

for a reason.

*So you have to believe
that,*

*in due time,
everything will be all right.*

The universe corrects itself.

*It will set you
on your own path,"* I said.

*"Maybe it was me.
Maybe I just wasn't enough . . ."* she said
as she continued to sob.

*"Don't ever
put yourself down.*

*You know
who you are.*

*You know
you offered the best versions*

of yourself to him.

*You know
you did your part.*

*You know
you fought*

*and fought
to make it work.*

You know you did.

*Sure,
maybe you weren't perfect.*

No one is.

*But don't you dare
ever say*

you weren't enough.

*You are enough.
You always were."*

WHEN THE RIGHT PERSON STEPS INTO YOUR LIFE LIKE A SUN, FULL OF LIGHT

Things will be better
with the right person.

You won't have to
remind them

of how you want
to be treated.

You won't have
to fight for their attention.

You won't feel alone.

You won't feel broken.
Empty.

As if
something is missing.

It'll be easy
with the right person.

Effortless.

And it'll just feel right.
You'll no longer feel

insecure

about the relationship.

You'll no longer worry.
It'll be beautiful.

Memorable.

And the wait
will be worth it.

The right person
will make you feel

at home.

And they will calm the storms
in your heart.

WHEN PEOPLE SHOW YOU HOW MUCH THEY CARE, YOU BOTH BECOME FLOWERS

They will find
time for you

if they care.

They will remember you.
They will make you feel

appreciated.

Make you feel
understood.

Loved. Needed.

No matter how hectic
their lives are,

if they really care . . .
they'll be there for you.
No matter what.

WHEN THE UNIVERSE IS COMPLETE, YOU KNOW YOUR PLACE—YOU KNOW WHO YOU ARE

I love
who I am

when I am with you.

I love
the way you make

me feel.

That's why
I need you.

That's why
I love you.

Because you make me
better.

You don't
only make feel

alive
in this universe
but you also

make me feel
like I am

a part of it.

And I am grateful
for that.

I am grateful
for you.

WHEN THE TIPS OF YOUR FINGERS TOUCH THE TIPS OF YOUR MAKER'S FINGERS ... THE REVELATIONS ARE UNCANNY

"I feel so empty," she said.

*"Like a part of me
is missing.*

*A little cold inside.
A little dead.*

A little lost.

*A little confused.
I just don't know*

*where
or how to start over.*

*Everything
is so fucked-up right now,"* she added.

At first,
I was happy

she finally broke up
with him.

She finally chose
herself

over him.

After all,
he did treat her kind of bad.

At least
from what she would tell me.

And from what
I saw,

those few times
I ran into them in public,

I was just glad
it was over.

Not because
I had feelings for her.

Or anything
like that.

But because
I just wanted to see her happy.

I just wanted
someone to love her.

To hold her.

To care for her.
To make her feel whole.

She had gone
through a series

of bad relationships
since the beginning,

and I had been there
to witness them all.

Very few
had potential

at first,
but in the end,
it's all the same.

"I think
it's okay to feel

this way, love.

I think.
Although you did
what was right

for you,

sometimes
choosing what's right

just hurts.

I also think,
and this might sound
strange,

but
in a strange way

I think
we leave a part of ourselves

with everyone
we open up to.

With everyone
we get vulnerable with.

That's why it hurts.

That's why
you feel empty sometimes.

You feel cold.
A little quiet.

A little lost.
Confused. Etc.

The more people
we love,

the more of ourselves
we lose.

But not all hope
is lost.

With everyone you love,
you also gain

something
in return.

Although
at first it may seem

as if
all is lost,

you feel gone,
but you are not gone.

You feel empty—broken,
but you are not empty.

You are not broken.

And you are definitely
not dead inside.

You are very much
alive.

Too much!

It is just,
right now,

you do not see it."

"It's just so hard," she said.

"Oh, I know it is.
We all know.

We have all been there.
But you know what?"

"What?"

"You will overcome it.
You will rise

to the surface
again

and breathe.

You will,
because you've been here before.

You will,
because you've overcome

so many things
that have been even harder.

You're a survivor.
A lover.

A giver.

You have the whole
goddamned universe

inside of you
brewing.

Sparking.
Shining.

Collapsing
and rebuilding.

It is all in you.
In me.

In all of us."

A deep silence came over us.
It clouded

our entire atmosphere.

Or so
it felt like it.

"You'll be okay, love.
I know you will.

Believe me."

WHEN IT HURTS SO BAD AND YET YOU STILL FIND IT WITHIN YOU TO SURVIVE

Sometimes
you give them your heart

and they give you
shit.

And sometimes
you hold on to them

a little longer

because you deeply
believe

they will change.

But that's not the case
for most.

You can't change
someone
when their heart
isn't there.

You can't help
someone

who doesn't want
to be helped.

And you can't love
someone

who doesn't want
to be loved.

Sadly,

this is the harsh reality
we go through

sometimes.

And sadly,
there aren't enough words

to write

what it is
we feel.

WHEN YOUR ARMS ARE TOO TIRED TO CARRY ALL OF THE PEOPLE YOU LOVE

It was midafternoon.

My dog was lying
on my lap

on a Friday,
and I decided to finally open

all the texts
from the night before.

One particular
message I received

compelled me
to write back.

As
I, too, was feeling
the same way.

The message said . . .

*"I wonder why I had to deal
with unreal people.*

Unforgiving people. Uncaring people.

Sometimes it feels
kinda like a curse."

My dog was heavy on my leg.
My other dog

jumped on the bed.

And I could feel this
stir

rise from the center
of my core.

It was my soul.

"I feel the same way, too.

I think
because people like you
and me
are too emotional.

Too empathetic with others.

We feel too much.

We care too much.
And when we don't get

that same level
of attention,

that same level
of respect,

we fall apart.

We want people
to love us

the same way
we love them.

We want them
to be like us.

To be a reflection
of our actions.

Of our own sentiments.

*But I have learned
through the years,*

*we can't expect
too much*

of those we love.

*We can't expect
them*

*to be the same way
we are*

with them.

*We are just
too different.*

*And it is not
in our nature*

*to want to change people.
It is not*

our place

to force them
to be anything, really.

We just expected
too much of them.

So much
that it crushes us

in the end
with disappointment.

With pain.
With suffering.

We care too much.
We love too much.

And I don't know
if that's a good

or bad thing.

*But we shouldn't
change*

*because they don't give us
what we need.*

*We shouldn't
let us feel*

*as if
we should care*

*a little less.
No.*

*We have to be
ourselves.*

*And if that's
the way we are,*

*and that's the way
they are,*

*then we must learn
to accept this fact.*

We are who we are,
and we shouldn't change

that
for no one.

We just have
to live with it

sometimes.

And set our hearts free.
Even if it feels

like a curse
sometimes."

I sounded bitter.
I know.

But sometimes
that's the way

I feel about things.
About people.

About family.
About life.

Sometimes I don't get
what I want.

The reaction
I want.

But I'm learning
to accept this.

I am learning
to let people

be

who they want
to be.

Sometimes
we hold on

because we think
we have to.

We put up
with the emotional abuse.

With all
the bullshit

they give us.

With all
the pain

they've inflicted.

And still
we hold on

because we think
we have to.

Because
we'll feel bad

if we decide to let go
and move on.

Because we have so much

history

together
and because

we're afraid of being alone.

Sometimes
we hold on

for the wrong reasons.

For reasons
we can't understand
ourselves.

We hold on
to the point . . .

where our hearts bleed
and bruise.

But there comes a time
when you must ask yourself

why.

Why are you still here?
Why do you take

all of this abuse?

Why do you stay
when you know

things can be better?
Why?

You're a lover.
You're a believer.

And I know
you want to believe
that they will change.

But they won't.
Deep down inside

you know
they won't.

Because, chance
after chance,

things just go back
to the way they were.

Things stay
the same,

and it hurts, love . . . I know.

But I think
you've been holding on

for far too long.

It's time to let go.
It's time to rest.
You've been exhausted
for so long.

It's time to move on
from all the things

you've held on to.

All the people
who've caused more harm

than good.

It's time to give up
on them.

It's time to move on.

You may feel broken
right now,

but you will find
a way to heal.

You always do.
You just can't
run away

from all the things
that hurt.

because you take them
with you,

no matter how far you go.

Therefore,
you have to fix yourself
from within

if you want peace.

Heal your heart.
Clear your thoughts

and feelings.

And focus
on what makes you happy.

Day by day.
And at your own pace.
You have to chip away
at what hurts.

Little by little.

And by the time you know it,
all of that weight

is off your shoulders.

Sadness is heavy
like that.

It'll keep you still.

Make things harder
to move on from.

But you have hope.
And friends.

And love.

And everything you need
to let go.

All you have
to do

is be brave
and find the courage

within yourself
to begin

and
to let go.

r.h. Sin

The day was breaking, and so was her heart. What is the point of love if it hurts this bad? Sorrow is all she's ever known. Lured into trust by lies, forced to believe in something that was never quite real. Who would have thought that a dream could become a nightmare so quickly and the reality of sadness could appear in the snap of a finger or, in this case, the crack of a heart? She's been here before, on the edge of a place that once felt like home, but even in her past experiences of heartbreak, this doesn't make it any easier; it never does. Sure enough, there are lessons and wisdom to be gained each time disappointment plagues the heart; each time she's forced to heal, the scar tissue hardens and makes it even more difficult to allow someone new in. Now, she's faced with an obstacle, a moment of dreadful clarity. The understanding that the love she thought she'd discover under the rubble of what had fallen before was just more of everything she'd been struggling to avoid.

"It may be tough now, but it'll get better by the morning," she whispers gently to herself, but no one knows which day that'll be and how long it'll really take to get over this familiar feeling of pain. "You tell someone what hurt you before, they listen intently, and they mirror the concern in your face, only to then hurt you in some of the same ways," she thinks to herself. The heart finds itself opening up, blooming toward the person who will never actually nurture it, but too often you only realize this in the end. Sadly, it is at the moment that something is finished that the truth comes spilling out, messy and dark, with no concern for how badly it'll hurt you.

One day, you awake from that feeling, still weary from the experience of being let down; the morning, once spent mourning, now becomes a foundation on which your future can be built. I guess the real war is that in-between place, the line in the sand of holding and letting go. The struggle of reaching the other end of heartbreak damages some of your belief in real love each time, but somehow you arrive here, still hopeful, searching for something that is better than what you've had—clinging to this idea that despite the presence of chaos, peace can be cultivated and maintained. You learn so much from the people who mean only to destroy you, lessons about who or what not to love from people you genuinely care for.

There was something about her; that "something" transcended words. She was a vision, one that you only get a glimpse of during deep meditation. She spoke with a soft strength, gentle and profound. Her whisper could wake the night, a beautiful call toward the morning. She was life happening to itself, more than a moment, something that could only be comprehended and adored over a lifetime. She's alone because nothing and no one has been brave enough to match the magnitude and power of the love that lives within her heart.

Whenever I was alone, I'd whisper to the night sky, "Come find me when you're done wasting your time on him . . ." I like to think that when you were weary, restless, and unable to sleep, you'd hear me calling out to you.

Sometimes a soul mate is just distracted by someone who can't love them. This is why it takes so long to find the right person. I know this from experience. In between the hurt and disappointment, you look up at the moon, and you think about your beloved and whether that love will ever find you . . .

The spine of your book is worn; the pages are
tattered and torn. So much of your story has
gone unheard. The suffering of your heart, a tale
of mistrust and neglect. Some of those pages
are soaked from the nights you've wept. And
yet a beautiful story is left to be told. You are a
collection of poetry; you are food for the soul.

———————

I'm sorry you thought it was okay to lose me.

—————————

I love you. Not for what you can do for me but for
what I'm willing to do for you.

someone who listens

someone loyal

someone considerate

someone kind

someone supportive

it's that simple

You see that bridge behind you? Destroy it.
There's no reason to go back there, and there is
no reason for the things you left behind to have a
way of reaching you.

———————

like the moon

when midnight arrives

you will find light

shining from within

_____

i think her tongue

was made of honey

sweet in everything she says

sweet is everything she's kissed

she's a summer song

the sun waltzing on her skin

the breeze whispering her name

and even as the night is over

the moon lingers in the morning sky

to catch a glimpse of the light

hitting her face

Sucks to be cheated on, but eventually you have to realize that the betrayal just means you get to find someone better. Someone worthy of your energy.

It's wild, suddenly becoming the best thing to ever happen to a person whenever I leave them. It's so strange how people wait until they lose a thing to love it.

When you betrayed me, you weren't just hurting
me; you were destroying your chance at love
and a future you didn't think you deserved.
Now, I look around, and I'm grateful to you for
abandoning me because your absence made room
for the love you were incapable of providing.

—————————

Your kindness is a superpower. It's beautiful;
it's attractive. That part of you—that part of you
that you've wasted on the wrong people—is
still valuable, and I hope you find the one who
deserves it.

———————————

If they're struggling to love you back, let them go.

_____

someone who only wants you

someone who isn't entertaining others

while you're only focused on them

someone who isn't afraid to fall with you

someone who is brave enough to be vulnerable

someone who matches your ability to remain loyal

i hope you find them

_____

Sometimes you have to reach for yourself.
Sometimes the hero you've been searching for
lives within your own heart. There are a lot of you
who feel alone, and you shouldn't because YOU
have YOU, and YOU are more than enough.

_____

You're not being insecure; you're not overreacting. If that shit hurts, it hurts, and you don't have to pretend to be okay with it.

———————

You are RARE. Stop trying to find yourself in other people. Not everyone is built like you.

What's wild is that, in the process of trying to become a better version of yourself for the person you're with, you might find that the person you've become is no longer compatible with the person you tried to change for.

———————————

She's not everywhere, and she can't be with just anyone because she understands her value and the power of her presence.

No matter what gets said, people will treat you how they feel about you. Pay attention to the action, not the words.

_____

The sadness turns into anger, and that's when
people start to pay attention, but by then, it's
usually too late.

———————

In a safe relationship, you don't have to pretend to be okay with things you find inappropriate.

This year hasn't been easy; you might have
fallen a couple of times, but it's important to give
yourself credit for surviving everything meant to
tear you down. You may not be where you want
to be, but at least you're here.

_____

No man is ever too busy for a woman he feels is a priority in his life. If you are important to him, he will always find a way to show you. If you aren't, he'll just make excuses.

—————————

Peaceful romantic connections are rare.

_____

her sad eyes
show flickers
of hope
and moments
of strength

despite all the pain
she still sees true love
in her future

a beautiful vision
of everything
her heart deserves

———————

there will come a time

when you realize

that they are not listening

and this is when

you should begin

to walk away in silence

————————————

in a lonely world
i want to be
alone with you

———————

Throughout my life, I've had to accept that what is meant for me won't let me down. And that all the pain and betrayal happen for a reason. Let it hurt, then let go. Let it hurt, learn the lesson, and move on.

It's hard to see the blessing in being hurt by someone you love when you're in the middle of it, but in time you realize how much better life can be in the absence of people who do not deserve to be a part of your future.

Her beauty isn't loud; it's not trying too hard to be seen. Her beauty is calm, smooth, and effortlessly easy. Naturally profound.

———————————

So many good women are single right now because a lot of people don't know what real gold looks like. They don't know what a real blessing feels like. But it's okay, because a good woman is not for everyone.

_____

wild, loyal

strong, soft

you are the most exciting

idea of what love can be

don't settle

———————————

waiting for you
waiting for me
we're both distracted
by the idea
that we found something
in someone
who has nothing real
to show us

that uneasiness in your chest
is the same as the one
that lives here within me

it's a message that holds meaning
a sign that we have yet
to find one another
but one day or one night
we will

_____

fall in love with her kindness

and build a sweet future

———————

my hand between her thighs

my palm against her skin

the sun is setting

heaven at my fingertips

_____

eventually you recover

you then discover

that when in need of love

you become your lover

_____

after years of waiting

i found out that the thing

i'd been waiting for

was already with me

beneath skin and bone

————————

lips on skin
meditative medicine

but when she moved

the world stopped spinning

so that it could watch an angel fly

These were the things that often escaped me;
the very thing that I felt I deserved was the
hardest thing to capture. For most of my adult
life, I'd wanted to be loved in a way that wasn't
conditional. For so much of my life, I longed
for peace that couldn't be easily compromised.
I wanted these things so badly because, for the
majority of my childhood, these things were kept
from me by everyone I entrusted my life to. These
things were kept from me by the people I loved
the most.

There's this painful, bliss-like fever dream of
a moment when you finally realize the true
motivations for the things you long for the most.
You begin to realize that your heart's desire is
based upon how your childhood was constructed,
and once you get to that understanding, you're
fully willing to destroy what was built so that
you can build up something beautiful. You and
I just want the joy we deserve, and we are fully
committed to what needs to be done to achieve it.

———————————

You will not find peace comparing yourself to the
things you see in the world and online.

The fingers are puzzle pieces, the spaces in between made perfectly for the person who deserves to hold your hand. I know it hasn't been easy. You've held on to the wrong pieces for far too long, but I hope you find the one that fits. I hope you find the one who gives true meaning to the act of walking hand in hand.

————————————

Stop pretending to be okay with the things that
make your heart feel uneasy.

———————————

the smell of ocean water

the wind against your skin

the sound of crashing waves

the chance for peace to begin

the sand beneath your feet

it finds its way between your toes

your lips gently parted

your eyes are tightly closed

—————————

don't go back

to your ex

stop reaching for a door

that was built to be an exit

_____

this moment

the one in which

you are reading

these words

this moment

is the only moment

that matters

the calm you feel

right now

the reassurance

in your heart

as you now feel seen

and understood

stay here for a while

stay here with me

_____

we could've been great

but i'm trying to remember

that the most important thing

is what i have

and not what used to

belong to me

nothing about the love
you've been searching for
has been easy

there have been
plenty of fires
to put out

your battle scars are visible
many wounds are present

years of struggle
and disappointment
prolonged hopelessness
and regret

————————

i never mind the rain

i enjoy getting wet

whether it be the sky

or by her

_____

she got wet

i went swimming

capable of creating a sea

a woman made a diver out of me

_____

on nights
when i lie
restless
i long for
the meditation
between her thighs

my mind was not in the gutter
you see
my mind was thinking of drinking
tasting the sweet nectar
dripping from her flower

a wild meditation, moments of freedom
hidden away from the chaos
of the world
safe inside her garden

silence is a poem

the way it says everything

without saying anything at all

it could mean anything

and it depends on who

that silence is shared with

i know that sometimes your silence

is out of fear or even sadness

but in this moment

as you silently read these words

there is peace, and i'm grateful

you shared that with me

———————

Part of the problem is that your actions are not aligned with what you say. You see, you claim to want love, but you entertain people who need some sort of incentive to care for you. Listen, you can't love a person into loving you, and the purest love of all is one without condition. If unconditional love is what you crave, stay away from people who make you feel like you're hard to love.

A room full of people and still you are worth their undivided attention. I hope you find someone whose eyes do not wander because they're too busy focusing on you.

Don't waste another moment of your life on someone who makes you question whether or not you deserve the things you're asking for. Being single and alone will always be better than being in a relationship that makes you feel lonely.

_____

This realization that the people I've helped the
most, the people I've been the kindest toward,
the people I've always been there for are the
ones who have made me out to appear worthless.
It's funny how that works. It's sad that this has
happened.

Imagine doing everything for a person and they can't match the energy because they're too busy lending themselves to people who don't do half of what you do for them.

––––––––––––

It's hard to be careful when people are careless
with you.

My love is never-ending; it can transcend time.
Expand if need be, just as long as you need me.
My love, a profound expression, a blessing to
whoever can comprehend it. Always available to
the one who decides to cherish it. My love, too
big for small talk and empty promises. My love is
yours for as long as you allow it to be. My love,
our love.

This didn't make any sense. After all the sweet
nothings, all that was left was sour in our silence.
After everything I'd been through before you, I
shouldn't be surprised. I know the signs, the red
flags. The true color of deceit.

I'm flawed in many ways, but I think I have a superpower. I have this ability to be the most consistent thing in a lifetime if I'm allowed the opportunity to do so, and I think there are many of you reading this right now who share that same ability. My advice to you is to not let heartbreak change that. Don't let anyone who isn't for you change or distract you from the path leading to the one. Don't lose who you are because of someone who thought it was okay to lose you.

It's so easy to daydream about a life outside
your own, but it's important to be present and
to appreciate everything your life currently is.
I outgrew the part of me that looks over at the
way others live. I've outgrown the part of me
that dreams of something more while neglecting
what I already have. Be here, be present, be
now. Be here, because this is a beautiful start,
despite whatever obstacles you've faced. Never
want what someone else has, because you have
no idea what they had to do to get those things,
and oftentimes if you did you'd realize that FOR
YOU, IT ISN'T WORTH IT.

There is nothing more beautiful than the present
because it is here that you have life and the
opportunity to pursue more of your purpose. It
is here in this moment when most of what you
love and enjoy exists. Life is so fragile, yours and
my own. Tomorrow is not promised. Appreciate
where you are, and make it beautiful.

_____

When I was trying to show you something different, you didn't want it. My effort was wasted, and my devotion was never enough. I guess it takes time to see value in something you once had, especially when the thing you chose turns out to be nothing. I was always this, the thing you see, the thing you miss. I was always me, overlooked by you.

With maturity, you learn to appreciate the things you have in this life and the people in it. Don't be fooled by all these usernames, content, photos, and videos. You may think you have options, but most of those are not profound. Just ask anybody out there . . . there's not much but more of what you don't want. Should you ever meet someone who genuinely cares for your soul, someone who inquires about your last meal, someone who loves you through all your ups and downs and changes, someone who sees the version of you that YOU don't share on your feed, the part of you that most people have deemed unlovable, the part of you that most people force you to feel like you have to hide . . . if you find someone who loves every inch of you as if they've laid eyes on perfection, love them and never let them go, or at the very least, appreciate the fact that you have found heaven amid hell, peace in the middle of chaos.

I want only what is meant for me. I want only
to share my moments with someone who
understands the profound value of the present. I
only want what is sustainable, and all that I desire
is what will last. If it's not worth it, I don't want
it.

———————

Don't lose who you are because of someone who thought it was okay to lose you.

A focused woman is delightfully dangerous.

_____

You won't find diamonds distracting yourself
with stones.

————————————

People turn you cold and then criticize you for lacking warmth.

———————

Toxic people are draining. Not only that but they're also meant to distract you from living the life you feel you deserve.

———————

I have no room in my life for people who don't consider how their actions affect themselves or me.

———————

Healing doesn't always feel like healing.
Recovery hurts.

This is a sign: You know how you've wondered again and again if it's worth giving them another chance? It's not. People care for you not by words but with actions. Their actions are not rooted in love. It's time to let them go and set yourself free.

_____

Cheaters will always justify cheating until they get cheated on.

It's an act; don't trust it. All lies; don't believe it.

_____

I'm learning that, in order to cultivate a beautiful future, I must forgive those who have hurt me in the past.

_____

The heartbreak is just a transition to something better. You will get through this.

Oftentimes, "I miss you" is a form of manipulation. People lose you on purpose, and when they can't replace you, they claim it was a mistake.

———————

In loving you, I stopped loving myself.

_____

Save your feelings, thoughts, and ideas for people who care. Give silence to people who are not interested in what you have to say.

Being in a relationship with someone who has
never experienced a healthy relationship is
so difficult. It requires so much patience and
emotional energy. They treat you the way they've
been treated, and you somehow try to be the
difference, but it's not easy.

_____

When a man says, "I don't deserve you," to his partner, it's a confession of all the things he's doing in the dark, behind their back.

―――――――

there won't be
a next time
this first time
was the last

i thought this
was worth a lifetime
i believed
this would last

invested my heart
and every part of my soul
all for the chance
of together, growing old

i rearranged my whole life
i sacrificed what was
because for some reason
i believed this was love

and now all alone
in this room where i sit
four walls fully empty
because you never
gave me shit

and the people
they'll talk
who cheated?
why'd they quit?

but i'll say nothing
sit in silence
the whole time
feeling sick

this was never sustainable
i should have known it from the jump
picked your heart up from the rubble
should've left it in the dump

When someone cheats on you, that simply means that the person you're supposed to be with is still out there. Too often, because of childhood trauma and old wounds, we find ourselves choosing to hold on to inadequate partners. You must understand that there is always a reward in walking away from a person who doesn't deserve you. Most of the people you meet will just be lessons, obstacles, and distractions from all the things you know you deserve. Be grateful for the ones who show you what to avoid; be thankful for the ones who show you the way toward someone better.

———————

You were both an obstacle and a lesson. I'm so
happy I got over you.

———————

Scrolling as if she'd lost something behind the screen of her phone, her grip tightened as a heaviness crept up into her chest, she sat there, immersed in a moment of tears, looking out from her sad eyes like a child staring out into the rain from a window dressed in raindrops. Sadness had become her, weary from the discovery of several discouraging truths. Left alone to question how or what she did to deserve this pain in her chest, she wandered onto the profile of her emotional abuser, someone who she once believed would be the one never to leave her. This person was true love, or so she had thought, wiping away the tears as some managed to fall onto the screen.

The last few days have felt like weeks of misery, and though she saw the end coming, it was still difficult to grasp.

"How could the one who promised me forever become the one who didn't last?" she'd ask herself repeatedly, like a scratched vinyl skipping with difficulty to move forward.

Of course, this wasn't the first time she'd had her heart slashed down the center, but this felt different. The beginnings were slightly similar to all the things that begin beautifully, only to drip and run cold like December rain. There were flashes of hope, more than she'd ever experienced with a partner, and though this movie pretty much suffered the same ending, this particular script felt stronger than those that came before it.

In that cold room, lying beneath a full moon, she raised her arm, her skin slightly illuminated by the glow of the night sky, and whispered gently into the air of nothingness, "She's strong, but she's tired." These words had become a part of her, a tattoo, a telling of her life. A reminder of whom she'd been in the wake of disappointment, a message to herself from herself.

"I am strong, but I am tired!" she began to cry out, repeating profoundly until this self-assuring mantra became a lullaby. Her voice faded behind the hum of the night, her lips resting together as her eyes gave in to the heaviness of sorrow. She drifted into a dream, maybe a place where she could be happier than this. The heart began to rest in preparation for the battles of tomorrow.

That sea of conversation has dried itself to
nothing, a drought where an abundance of love
used to dwell. I sit near the shore, feet planted in
the sand, staring into the abyss of you. I could fill
the silence with my words, but I knew it wouldn't
matter. You stopped listening to me a long time
ago. This had always been evident by the way
you disregarded my feelings, constantly finding
yourself in a position to hurt me, pretending it
was a mistake, but it would turn out that a lot of
thinking went into the things you chose to do.
You made decisions solely based on your own
satisfaction, knowingly taking part in what would
render me dissatisfied. Constantly, I found myself
questioning what I meant to you. I was confused
by the illusion of love, while your lies supported
my delusions of you.

I miss the old you. The person you've become
has been a result of walking backward. You've
descended into a pit of all things I've been
avoiding. It's a shame that you couldn't live up
to your promises, lying about who you intend to
be. And now I'm left alone, holding a mask of
everything you pretend to be. The disguise no
longer fits; this was an oversize dream.

I think you can tell when something is off or when they're distracted . . . possibly by someone else. It's like they're always engaging in something outside of you, and you wonder what it is. You want to ask, but you don't because you know they'll just lie to you.

That's the beginning of the end, but it's also the beginning of a new path, one that leaves more room for self-love and reflection. Room to grow, to learn, and to build up courage to leave them behind. That moment and every moment after, every moment of neglect and disappointment, is a revelation that proves to you that there is someone better out there for you.

To anyone who has been tricked into staying with someone who has already begun to leave, I hope you know that it is never too late to walk away from that person, and it is never too late to rediscover yourself and your strength. It'll be tough, the roads ahead, but you are built for this, and you will overcome this feeling of defeat and sadness.

One of the toughest lessons I've learned in my life is that you can do most things right, care for a person deeply, show up in a way that no one has, and they'll still find an excuse to wrong you, to betray, to lie, and to disappoint you. It took me years to realize that no amount of good means anything to a person who has neither respect for you nor respect for themselves. There are so many good, loyal, and honest people out here in the world, and I hope they all find each other, no matter how difficult.

We are surrounded by sheep pretending to be
wolves, people who follow their temporary
desires for more of nothing . . . badly represented
by themselves and their actions, aggressive in
their pursuit to ruin their own lives and yours.
Claiming they love you while treating you as if
they hate you. And when you discover their ways,
they gaslight you and force you to feel insecure
or "crazy." I've learned from my own experience
that the only way out is through them. See them
for the frauds they are and replace them with the
love you have in your own heart. Move forward,
and resist the urge to allow them to distract you
from the person who will love you in a genuine
way.

In this life, I learned that even when hurt, even
when tired and confused, you will always end
up in a better situation, living a better life than
anyone who has tried to destroy you. The truth is
you just have to figure out how to put them in the
past.

Through these lessons, I have learned to love the
act of letting go, because this is the way toward
the love you deserve.

You have to be more than just there. Be present.
The love you proclaim has to feel like it; your
actions give meaning to the things you say.
Don't just be with someone for the sake of not
being alone. Do not waste your time using empty
people to fill a void. Don't make decisions when
you're angry or sad. Think before you act. Think
to yourself, "Will this make me a better person?
Will my life improve? Is there a lesson here, an
opportunity for growth?" Do not continue down
the same roads that have always led you to a dead
end, and do not entertain old relationships that
keep you from experiencing new and meaningful
things. Love yourself; you have to learn to love
yourself even when those you love refuse to love
you back, and you have to be okay with being
alone. I need you to understand that sometimes
absence is a blessing. Sometimes being
abandoned just means you dodged a bullet.

r.h. Sin index

My love is never-ending; it can transcend time.   163

No man is ever too busy for a woman he feels is a priority
    in his life.   127

No matter what gets said, people will treat you how they
    feel about you.   123

nothing about the love   152

Oftentimes, "I miss you" is a form of manipulation.   181

on nights   155

Part of the problem is that your actions are not aligned with
    what you say.   157

Peaceful romantic connections are rare.   128

People turn you cold and then criticize you for
    lacking warmth.   172

Save your feelings, thoughts, and ideas for people who
    care.   183

Scrolling as if she'd lost something behind the screen of
    her phone, her grip tightened as a heaviness crept up into
    her chest, she sat there, immersed in a moment of tears,
    looking out from her sad eyes like a child staring out into
    the rain from a window dressed in raindrops.   190

she got wet   154

she's a summer song   111

She's not everywhere, and she can't be with just anyone
    because she understands her value and the power of her
    presence.   122

silence is a poem   156

So many good women are single right now because a lot of
    people don't know what real gold looks like.   135

someone who listens   107

someone who only wants you   117

Sometimes you have to reach for yourself.   118

Stop pretending to be okay with the things that make your
    heart feel uneasy.   147

Sucks to be cheated on, but eventually you have to realize that the betrayal just means you get to find someone better.   112

That sea of conversation has dried itself to nothing, a drought where an abundance of love used to dwell. 192

The day was breaking, and so was her heart.   100

The fingers are puzzle pieces, the spaces in between made perfectly for the person who deserves to hold your hand.   146

The heartbreak is just a transition to something better.   180

There was something about her; that "something" transcended words.   102

there will come a time   130

there won't be   186

The sadness turns into anger, and that's when people start to pay attention, but by then, it's usually too late.   124

These were the things that often escaped me; the very thing that I felt I deserved was the hardest thing to capture.   144

the smell of ocean water   148

The spine of your book is worn; the pages are tattered and torn.   104

This didn't make any sense.   164

This is a sign: You know how you've wondered again and again if it's worth giving them another chance?   176

this moment   150

This realization that the people I've helped the most, the people I've been the kindest toward, the people I've always been there for are the ones who have made me out to appear worthless.   160

This year hasn't been easy; you might have fallen a couple of times, but it's important to give yourself credit for surviving everything meant to tear you down.   126

Beautiful Sad Eyes, Weary Waiting for Love copyright © 2023 by r. h. Sin and Robert M. Drake. All rights reserved. Printed in China. No part of this book may be used or reproduced in any manner whatsoever without written permission except in the case of reprints in the context of reviews.

Andrews McMeel Publishing
a division of Andrews McMeel Universal
1130 Walnut Street, Kansas City, Missouri 64106

www.andrewsmcmeel.com

23 24 25 26 27 SDB 10 9 8 7 6 5 4 3 2 1

ISBN: 978-1-5248-8506-9

Library of Congress Control Number: 2023933576

Editor: Patty Rice
Art Director: Diane Marsh
Production Editor: Elizabeth A. Garcia
Production Manager: Julie Skalla

ATTENTION: SCHOOLS AND BUSINESSES
Andrews McMeel books are available at quantity discounts with bulk purchase for educational, business, or sales promotional use. For information, please e-mail the Andrews McMeel Publishing Special Sales Department: sales@amuniversal.com.